Another Interesting Year

Adventures and Misadventures of the Fox family
told in Twenty Years of Christmas Letters

By Maru
&
Bill Fox

The Three Tomatoes Book Publishing
6 Soundview Rd.
Glen Cove, NY 11542
www.thethreetomatoespublishing.com

Copyright © 2020 by Maru and Bill Fox

All rights reserved. No part of this book may be reproduced in any form or by any electronic or mechanical means including information storage and retrieval systems, without permission in writing from the publisher. The only exception is by a reviewer, who may quote short excerpts in a review. For permission requests, please address The Three Tomatoes Publishing.

Published November 2020
Printed in the United States of America

ISBN: 978-1-7353585-7-4
Library of Congress Cataloging-in-Publication Data
2020922229

Illustrations, cover and interior design by Tony Iatridis

All company and/or product names may be trade names, logos, trademarks, and/or registered trademarks and are the property of their respective owners.

Advance Praise

"Hilarious! Every sentence makes you laugh. Reading the adventures of the Fox family is a gift you will want to give to all your friends. You have to keep reading: will the police mix-ups continue? Will Bill return to the Oprah show? Will Tobi (the dog) be the only family member prescribed valium? This the story of a real family with a real sense of humor. If you like to laugh, you will LOVE this book."

~ *Mary Jordan, Pulitzer Prize winning journalist*

"Riotous, warm-hearted, unique and fun, *Another Interesting Year* will make you count your blessings, including having 'met' the one-of-a-kind Fox family through this thoroughly entertaining compilation of twenty years of their hilarious Christmas letters."

~ *Jennie Fields, author Atomic Love*

"Vulnerable, uplifting and endearing often with plenty of slapstick comedy routines for a quick laugh. The self-deprecating humor is a joy. In an age when too many people overrate their importance, the simplicity of sharing our vulnerable side as if we were all having a cup of coffee at the kitchen table makes this an awesome read."

~*Barbara Longué, Best Selling Author and Business Coach*

"I've known the Foxes for over twenty years and I long ago fell for their funny, witty and warm annual Christmas letter. A special gift to all us about the joys in the ups and downs of everyday life.

~Joanne Davis, Co-CEO SCAN International"

"Ever get those long boring Christmas letters with a lot of minutiae you could care less about? Well, not so with Bill and Maru Fox's annual letter. It's pure merriment that's a cross between something out of The Pink Panther and the adventures of Jacques Cousteau."

~Jim Speros, Retired Chief Marketing Officer,
Fidelity Investments.

Dedication

This book is dedicated to Ali and Billy, instrumental partners on our often-crazy life journey. Thank you for being the awesome kids that you are and especially for being such good sports in our misadventures. We love you.

Table of Contents

2001 1
2002 4
2003 10
2004 16
2005 22
2006 26
2007 30
2008 34
2009 40
2010 46
2011 52
2012 58
2013 64
2014 70
2015 76
2016 82
2017 88
2018 92
2019 98
2020 104
Acknowledgments 108
About the Foxes 109

Another Interesting Year

CHRISTMAS 2001

To All Our Friends,
We hope this letter finds you all doing well. It was another "interesting year" for the Fox family full of intrigue, new schools, new jobs, weight gain, weight loss and the traditional Fox hospitalization. Yes, it was another typical year for the Fox family!

Maru had a milestone year. She threw the towel into the ring where her kick boxing career was concerned. She was spending more time at the chiropractor's office than the ring, so she opted for that other Mexican pastime, figure skating. Yes, our little Maru is twirling, jumping, gliding, and she even does some of these things on the ice. She took up skating as a way to spend more time with the family. Billy has decided he wants to be a hockey player when he grows up and Ali has been doing very well with her skating lessons; hence, Maru decided to brave the frozen water and hasn't looked back—mostly because she has not learned to turn around. She also hit the big "4-0" this year. This was celebrated with an "adult" weekend in New York, which was wonderful. We succeeded in "painting the town red, white and blue," just as Mayor Rudy Giuliani has asked—anything for the city we admire and love so much.

Ali turned five in April and started kindergarten this year. She has become quite the little lady. Her teacher has given her a stellar report during her first parent-teacher conference, but he did ask us where her "off" switch was—shy she is not! In addition to ice skating she enjoys ballet and loves to sing; she can break into a patriotic song of your choice at a moment's notice; clearly the focus of the school's music teacher.

Billy turned three in October and entered big boy nursery school and goes each day for a glorious two and a half hours. He spends the rest of his day practicing every contact sport imaginable. If the odds are that you are likely to break a bone doing it, he loves it. His number one favorite sport is hockey. He has asked Santa for a new hockey stick, skates, and a helmet. Bill has asked Santa for low cost dental insurance. Currently, Billy spends the afternoon hitting slap shots in the kitchen. Bill encourages him as he has heard there are great scholarships for hockey players. Maru on the other hand feels it would be cheaper to pay tuition rather than replacing all the glassware and appliances in the kitchen every year. They are currently doing the math.

Bill was the designated hospital patient this year. He had a double hernia (they offered a two for one special, so he figured what the hell) and landed in the hospital for what was a routine, but painful experience. He also had a major case of conjunctivitis and salmonella, so it was a relatively mild medical year for him. On the job front he remains very happy at his agency, despite a challenging year for the advertising business. No marathons this year (enough is enough), but he continues to run regularly to the amazement of friends and family alike.

The big event for 2001 is Maru and Bill's tenth anniversary

that they will be celebrating in style this December. They will renew their vows at that ever so reverent locale, "The Viva Las Vegas Wedding Chapel" in Las Vegas. Elvis lives! And he will officiate as they re-pledge their wedding vows in front of family, friends, and several other visitors in line to tie the knot, after meeting over a martini at the roulette table. As you can see, they decided on a low-key subdued affair.

On the whole, 2001 was a very good year to us and we have much to be thankful for. With so many lives lost senselessly on September 11th including several people we knew, we count our blessings that our immediate family is safe. We will never forget the brave souls that were lost, and we will always remember with pride how strangers became neighbors and united to help. It made us very proud to be New Yorkers.

To all our dear friends, we wish you God's blessings for a happy holiday season and peaceful and prosperous 2002.

Bill, Maru, Ali, and Billy

Another Interesting Year

CHRISTMAS 2002

To All Our Friends,

We hope this letter finds you all doing well. It was another "interesting year" for the Fox family. Maru and Bill got married for the third time to each other at the conclusion of 2001; the first one made us legal, the second made us married in the eyes of God (and the eyes of our parents) and the third one made us look ridiculous, but we can highly recommend renewing your wedding vows at the Viva Las Vegas Wedding Chapel. We were joined by friends, family, and total strangers as we pledged to love each other (and our hound dog) tenderly in front of The King and millions more who watched live via the internet. (Ok, maybe it was hundreds more who logged on by accident looking for some Elvis memorabilia, but that does not sound dramatic enough). The bride and groom looked radiant in matching pink boa and vest, chosen to match the pink Cadillac they arrived in for the ceremony. The wedding was every parent's dream.

However, as wild as that was, 2002 will be remembered for the wedding that wasn't. We entered 2002 with much anticipation of the wedding of Maru's younger sister, Rocio. Well the wedding was called off a couple of weeks before the wedding—a little issue came up that made her realize that this was not the man for her—he was already married. There was shock, there were tears, there was disbelief, there was the honeymoon that was already paid for, so Rocio went on it anyway (with her mother, not the bigamist). Off to Europe they went to forget about the good for nothing %^&*$! They returned refreshed and content— it is amazing what some shopping in Italy can do to put your life back in perspective.

Ali turned six in April and started first grade. She is doing wonderfully in school and Maru and Bill are happy she is off to a good start. Her teacher gave her a very nice report during her first parent-teacher conference, and we hope it is one of many to come. She is also doing extremely well with ice skating. She won a bronze medal in her first competition (you would have thought she won an Olympic Gold Medal with the way we all carried on) and she will be skating her second solo in a skating exhibition at Christmas. She also enjoys ballet, reading, screeching at a high, piercing pitch and painting her brother all sorts of colors. Overall, we are very proud of her—usually.

Billy turned four in October and continues to enjoy nursery school. All his friends are named Michael, so Maru never knows whom he wants to have a play date with, and it is usually not the one she thinks it is. He is still committed to a hockey career and still spends his day practicing slap shots in the kitchen when he is not practicing on the ice. He was in a Snowplow Sam class (think babysitting kids with skates on) when the Super Tot Hockey Coach spotted him since he was already skating backwards and pulled him into his class, so now he is the youngest hockey student in the school, the quickest skater in the group, and the only one who brings a teddy bear to the rink with him (thank God he is the fastest!).

2002

Maru continues her passion for ice-skating; who would have thought? Her proudest achievement came in early November when her teacher told her that she needed to upgrade her skates to be able to do the more advanced moves. She was so excited she couldn't sleep for a week. (Bill couldn't sleep either when he found out how much the new skates cost). She took up skating to spend more time with the family and now the family has to go the ice rink if they want to spend time with her.

Bill is the Fox family skating coach, which is a glorified title for the person responsible for getting everyone to the rink on time; getting everyone's skates on and off; and taking snack orders. He remains happy at the same ad agency, but it has been an extremely challenging year for the advertising business. He (and everyone else in the ad industry) is hoping for a much better 2003. He also ran enough New York Road Runners Races to qualify for the 2003 New York Marathon, so next year will be dedicated to preparing for his second marathon (even though he swore that he would never run another one).

We will be spending the holidays in New York this year and welcoming Maru's entire immediate family for the holidays—14 people will be in our house for two weeks. It will be joyous, family oriented, and a once in a lifetime experience (that's because we will never let this happen again). Maru's family is wonderful and they are great house guests, but two weeks of anyone living in your house that you are not legally obligated to, can drive the most sedate person to heavy doses of Valium after a few days. Therefore, in Bill's case, Maru has insisted he pop a few as they announce, "Now arriving at gate 14, AeroMexico flight 604 from Mexico City."

On the whole, 2002 was very good to us and we have much to be thankful for. To all our dear friends, we wish you God's blessings for a happy holiday season and peaceful and prosperous 2003.

Bill, Maru, Ali, and Billy

2002

Another Interesting Year

CHRISTMAS 2003

To All Our Friends,
We hope that this letter finds you all doing well. It was another "interesting year" for the Fox family. We concluded 2002 with the visit of Maru's entire family. Fourteen people for two weeks. We were apprehensive to say the least and were braced for another Alamo, but it honestly was a great time. The only incident was when Maru's mother fell down our front stairs and landed in a snow drift during the Christmas blizzard of '02.

She had insisted that there is a Chinese proverb that says that a "good smoke" helps the digestion after a big Christmas dinner (would any of our Chinese friends like to set the record straight?) and went out on the front porch, after fighting off her children and husband who had not heard of that Chinese proverb, and had her smoke. Maru went to check on her about twenty minutes after she went out for her digestive smoke and all she could see were her mother's feet in a snow drift. Hysterically she called the rest of us to dig her out and we are happy to report she was fine and still puffing away when rescued. Bill is convinced there is the foundation of a Cohen Brother's movie in there somewhere. And if that scene was not enough for a movie script the matter of Maru's parents' marriage is.

During our annual summer pilgrimage to Mexico, Maru's parents dropped a bombshell (even for her family). Over dinner to "celebrate" Bill's departure from Mexico and mourn the fact the Maru and the kids were leaving, Maru's very proper, Catholic school, nuns in habits educated, Virgin de Guadalupe medal wearing mother announced that she was never legally married to the man she has called her husband for the past forty-three years and Bill learned he married a bastard; the shame of it. When Bill and the other "children-in-laws" finished laughing (a good hour and a round of after dinner drinks later) we learned the sorry truth. It seems that Maru's parents went through a marriage ceremony, but her mother had listed what she thought was her legal name (yet, another twist to the movie script) to find out forty-three years later when working on an updated will that she was not who she thought she is (was?). Confused now? Well, so was the registry office in Mexico which is why they called the last forty-three years off. Viva Las Vegas Wedding Chapel, here we come again!

Closer to home, we are happy to report that Bill regained his form and succeeded in recapturing his title of Fox family hospital victim in 2003. He broke his arm in two places ice skating with the family. In classic Bill Fox fashion, he jumped onto the ice with one of his skate guards on and voila, the championship was his on January 18th, and the title held up for the remainder of the year. Oh yeah, and he successfully completed the New York Marathon on behalf of the Multiple Sclerosis Society in November; great experience, respectable time, wonderful crowds; never again (really this time)!

Ali turned seven in April and is now a very happy second

grader. She continues to do well in school and Maru and Bill are thrilled with the quality of the education. She is also doing extremely well with ice skating. She won the Gold Medal in her last competition (we see Mexican Olympic glory in 2014) and she will be skating her fourth solo exhibition at Christmas to the tune, *All I want for Christmas is my two front teeth*—a look at a recent photo will show the inspiration for that choice. She also made a huge breakthrough in ballet this year and will be appearing in the Westchester Ballet's performance of *The Nutcracker*. Her first professional appearance with contracts and waivers signed, the whole nine yards. So, Bill is still baffled by why this professional, tickets need to be purchased in advance performance, still wound up costing him several hundred dollars.

Billy turned five in October and entered kindergarten. He is so happy to be in big boy school and if he is happy, Maru is ecstatic. Billy has made a host of new friends and is into soccer and basketball, not to mention his promising hockey career, but then tragedy struck…He woke up on Sunday, November 23rd and announced that he would not be going to hockey practice that morning and may never ever again. The Earth shook, his coach took to his bed, and Bill started a college fund as the hopes of a hockey scholarship faded quickly. We all hope this "condition" is temporary but will keep you updated.

Maru has used her newfound few hours of freedom with Billy's newfound confinement in school to get back to the gym. Spin classes, aerobics, hip-hop dancing, and boxing are new passions. She continues to be a glorified taxi driver in the afternoon, but for a few golden hours during the day she is free! In her spare time, she volunteers for the church, takes Billy's class on nature walks, Bill to the Emergency Room, and manages to keep us happy and our family running like clockwork.

We will be spending the holidays in Mexico this year and will be meeting the newest member of the Vidaña family, Juan Pablo, Maru's brother's infant son who was born on November 3rd, Maru's birthday. There are no plans because we will be in Mexico, so what good are plans anyway? So, we are taking a new tactic and have announced that we are going to "go with the flow" and be spontaneous. Maru's family is scared to death as they have never heard of Bill's name and spontaneity used in the same sentence, so they are busy making plans for us.

On the whole, 2003 was very good to us and we have much to be thankful for.

To all our dear friends, we wish you God's blessings for a happy holiday season and peaceful and prosperous 2004!

Bill, Maru, Ali, and Billy

2003

Another Interesting Year

CHRISTMAS 2004

To All Our Friends,
We hope that this letter finds you all doing well. It was another "interesting year" for the Fox family. Bill had a new job offer stuffed into his Christmas stocking last year (thank you, Santa!). It was a great job opportunity to manage the in-house ad agency for a large financial firm, a significant agency in its own right within a well-run, extremely successful company working with a great group of people. The hitch— the family need to move to the Boston area: where lives the dreaded Red Sox (remember, Maru's mother mortgaged her home to scalp tickets from Mexico for a Yankees Word Series Game); where it snows by Thanksgiving (remember Mexican Maru who wears a turtleneck when there is a cool summer breeze); where the people speak a whole different language (remember, it took the family years to master their own form of Spanglish).

Well, the job was too good to pass up, so the ever adaptable Fox family put a For Sale sign on the house we loved; increased our life insurance since there was the added threat that a Sox fan would pick one of us off; bought thermal underwear; signed up for intensive Bostonian language classes; moved to Medfield, Massachusetts; and WE LOVE IT!

The moving van had barely been packed when the kids switched allegiance to the Red Sox; the people of Boston are the only people outside of Mexico, worldwide who can say

Maru's name correctly "Maaaru" (who knew the Boston accent was really Spanglish?); and the weather has been milder than New York (thus far).

The move went characteristically interesting for us. The house went on the market in February and we received no suitable offers for almost three months, despite everyone telling us that the place would sell in minutes, even with a plastic statue of St. Joseph buried in our backyard as we were told he helps "close house deals miraculously." We did not notice the fine print that St. Joe works better in warmer weather, so we panicked needlessly because with the spring thaw, St. Joseph worked his magic, we mean miracle, and the games began.

Three families entered into a bidding war (love a knockdown, drag down fight to our benefit). The winning couple was our personal favorite, not just because they offered the most money, but they seemed like they would fit in best with the neighborhood and we loved our neighbors.

Next came the physical move which went relatively smoothly until one of the workers tripped in the attic while bringing down some Christmas ornaments and fell through the ceiling onto the second floor—all this while the new owners were having coffee with us in the kitchen. The movers barricaded the stairs with a dresser until the new owners left and kind of put a gag on the worker who fell and was yelling out in pain, so that no one could hear him. We truly live for a dull moment. Fortunately, the worker's ego was hurt more than his body it turns out. The ceiling was easily fixed, and no ornaments were broken, so all good.

2004

Overall, the family is doing great. Billy was born to be in New England. He is back to hockey and plays three days a week and is already using expressions like "wicked cool." Ali had the toughest adjustment. She missed her friends and had to adjust to a new school, but now she is doing fine and has made some very nice new friends. She is taking a break from figure skating after several successful competitions last year (the Mexican Olympic Committee is in a panic as they fear they are losing their one and only potential star). But we are happy to report that she has found an even more expensive passion, horseback riding. So, on Saturday mornings we run from the skating rink to the horseback riding ring all before most normal people have had their morning coffee. Honestly, what is it with all these activities? The only supervised activities Maru and Bill had was when some chain-smoking mom in the neighborhood loaded twelve of us into her station wagon and drove us to the movies.

This is the year of family reunions. Bill's mom treated his brother and his entire family to a cruise this summer. It was the first time the Fox family had spent more than three hours together in twenty-five years and we had a blast. Next up, we will be spending Christmas in Mexico this year visiting "Maaaru's" family, much to Bill's anxiety. It is not that he does not enjoy the Mexican side of the family, he does, but travelling internationally at Christmas time is like a contact sport. But there is a lot to celebrate. Maru's mom turns seventy on Christmas day and we will be meeting the newest member of the Vidaña clan, Sofia, Irish twin daughter of Maru's brother (born nine months, one day apart from her older brother—oh come on guys, what were you thinking? Or not thinking?).

On a sad note, our beloved dog of fourteen years, Prisci, died soon after she moved to Medfield. She went peacefully, but we all miss her. That loss aside, 2004 was another year of many blessings and we have much to be thankful for.

To all our dear friends, we wish you God's blessings for a happy holiday season and peaceful and prosperous 2005!

Bill, Maru, Ali, and Billy

2004

Another Interesting Year

CHRISTMAS 2005

To All Our Friends,

We hope this letter finds you all doing well. It was another "interesting year" for the Fox family. The big news this time around is the renovation of our house.

We bought an ugly house. We knew the place had great potential when we bought it, but it was ugly—a poor imitation of the Brady Bunch house ugly; a wake up in the morning and scream, "What were we thinking ugly." But we made a low offer that wasn't refused, and with faith that it did have potential, we entered into the brave under world of renovation. And we are thrilled with the results and so are the folks that live nearby. People (many people) used to come up to us and say, "You bought an ugly house." Other people would just tell us "Good luck with the renovation of that ugly house," while they jogged by or walked their dog. Now most people say that they cannot believe that we saw such potential in such an ugly house, and we are flattered—we bought the swan.

The end result is much better than we imagined, and we owe much to the architect and the contractor. (Okay, when have you ever heard anyone praise their contractor? The only time we have heard folks mention their contractor "after" the job was to complain about what wasn't done and then only through their lawyer). They understood our vision (basically make it not ugly) and created a home that we are thrilled with. Now of course there were the typical Fox events that occurred during the gutting and reconstruction. The most memorable was the day Bill received a call from our home security company. It went like this:

"Mr. Fox, this is your security company, we are calling to tell you we got a credible signal that your house is on fire. We have sent the fire department. Good luck and good-bye."

Bill put down the phone and decided to take it a step at a time. First of all, he looked at his watch; it was early afternoon, so the kids were in school—a good thing. He called home and no one picked up, not even the answering machine—made sense since the house was on fire the wires may have burned.

He called Maru on her cell phone, went right into voicemail—made sense since she was probably calling the fire department to make sure they were on their way.

He called the contractor's office and was told that there was "a lot of commotion at the house." Made sense since a fire would qualify as a lot of commotion.

He called the foreman and asked if the house was on fire and was told, "No, but it was a good thing that the ambulance came." Bill swallowed hard and asked (ok, screamed), "What the hell is going on!!??"

That's when he was told that two members of the demolition crew (Dumb and Dumber) had cut through a set of live wires and so while the house was not on fire, their hair was. The electricity was reconnected the same day and the last we heard from the dynamic demolition duo was that they were back on the job destroying other ugly homes.

Overall, the family is doing well, and we all continue to

love living in Massachusetts. Billy is in first grade and playing every sport imaginable, but his passion remains hockey. His team recently won a local championship as the clear underdog and it was the highlight of his life. Ali is in fourth grade. It was a tough adjustment for her and has wished death to "whoever invented homework" on numerous occasions—truth is that if she spent half the time doing her homework versus complaining she would be done in less time than she complains about it (get the math?). Nevertheless, she is doing very well. Her passion continues to be horseback riding and she is the only member of the family that finds that sport appealing. Billy is allergic to horses, Maru went riding once, hurt her back and swore never again, and Bill sees no scholarship potential in it; other than that, the family supports her 100%

Maru thoroughly enjoys life in Medfield and continues to be the glue that holds the family together. She has enjoyed redecorating the transformed house and has made a lot of new friends. Bill continues to love his job and looks forward to work every day. The only hiccup for the Fox's was Bill's brain tumor, but aside from that it was an incredibly good year. Bill did sign up for speed skating lessons (yes, spandex and all) so Maru is not quite convinced that the surgery was as successful as the neurosurgeon claims. She has requested another MRI.

2005 was another year of many blessings (and successful surgeries) and we have much to be thankful for.

To all our dear friends, we wish you God's blessings for a happy holiday season and a peaceful and prosperous 2006!

Bill, Maru, Ali, and Billy

Another Interesting Year

CHRISTMAS 2006

To All Our Friends,

We hope that this letter finds you all doing well. It was another "interesting year" for the Fox family.

We started the year welcoming the newest member of the Fox family, Tobi, a little white dust mop of a thing that thinks he is a Retriever and is a lot of fun. We were told that Billy is allergic to everything that moos, barks, or meows so we set upon getting one of the so-called hypo-allergenic dogs. After some careful research on both the breeds and the price tags, we settled on the Bichon-poo, French for "high priced mutt that does not shed." He is a great dog, and the family loves him. We are also happy to report that he has been at the vet eight times since we got him—truly meant to be a member of the Fox family! Oh, and recent allergy tests showed the only thing that Billy is not allergic to is dogs, so we could have gotten a cheaper mutt.

Billy is in second grade and still whacking hockey pucks when he isn't whacking Ali. Ali is in fifth grade and still enjoys horseback riding and challenging just about everything we say. She is a born negotiator who's destined to make a killing as a lobbyist on Capitol Hill.

Maru and Bill took an interesting trip this year in May. They walked the last one hundred miles of the Camino de Santiago in northern Spain. Maru's dad dreamed this up as something he wanted to do for his seventy-fifth birthday.

Another Interesting Year

Maru's mom called crying that her crazy husband wanted to walk a hundred miles and she wanted us to talk him out of "his death march." Somehow, rather than talking him out it, he talked us into it. So, Bill and Maru bought backpacks, good hiking shoes and started to train two hours every day and eight hours a day on the weekends. Who else trains for their vacation?

The Camino is an old pilgrimage across the top of Spain to where the remains of the Apostle St. James are alleged to be buried. Droves including royalty flocked to the discovery from the time of Charlemagne and St. Francis of Assisi. We met others who were talked into this by their crazy fathers from all over the world. At one-point Bill spoke Japanese with a group of pilgrims from Kyoto, while Maru spoke French to a group from Toulouse, while Maru's dad entertained some cows with his harmonica. Yes, we are a worldly group. Most people walk one hundred miles in five days and lose fifteen pounds, but we gained five (thanks to the wine and paella). Maru's dad told us as we were concluding the Camino that a wonderful by-product of the trip was that our souls received a clean slate. Seems that all your sins are absolved when you walk the Camino, and we received a certificate at the Cathedral de Santiago declaring our "purity." Damn, the fun we would have had if we knew beforehand!

We are not sure who wins the medical patient award this year. Maru came down with viral meningitis, but they put Bill in the hospital for it. Two people in Bill's office were diagnosed at the same time as Maru, so Bill was quickly labeled

2006

"patient zero" and was whisked off to the hospital. After a million uncomfortable tests, Bill was informed that viral meningitis is not contagious. Maru got an aspirin and was told to sleep it off. Bill got triaged in the emergency room for something he did not have. Oh, and the two employees actually only had headaches in the end.

In typical fashion, we are concluding the year with a bang. Bill was at the office a week ago when Maru called from her cell phone sobbing. With each breath all she could blurt out between sobs was "Honey I killed it!" In the background Bill could hear Ali wailing, "We are going to hell!" and Billy yelling "We are going to jail!" Then Bill, with surprising calmness, inquired what it was they killed? Considering the reaction to the incident from the murderers, Bill was relieved to hear it was just a deer. Fortunately, no one was hurt, except the deer, the car is repaired, and no one is in jail. Jury is still out on whether they will go to hell.

We are looking forward to Maru's sister's wedding in the spring. Some of you may recall that her last marriage was called off at the last minute when she found out that the guy she was going to marry was already married (snitty little detail). The new man of her dreams, Sergio, seems like a keeper. Nice guy, not married, and loves her dearly.

2006 was another year of many blessings and we have much to be thankful for.

To all our dear friends, we wish you God's blessings for a happy holiday season and a peaceful and prosperous 2007!

Bill, Maru, Ali, and Billy

Another Interesting Year

CHRISTMAS 2007

To All Our Friends,
It was another interesting year for the Fox family full of good friends, family weddings, weight gain, weight loss and hospitalizations. On second thought, it was a relatively normal year (except the weight loss part).

Bill continues to work at the same company, and all goes well. He is also happy to report that he kept his hospitalization streak going in 2007. He had a painful cramp at the office so his assistant called the doctor (the only assistant who keeps her boss's doctor's number on speed dial). The doctor thought it might be a kidney stone, so he sent Bill to the emergency room where he was diagnosed with diverticulitis.

Okay, we did not know what that was either; it is an acute swelling of the intestines. They admitted him and said he would be fine in three days after some heavy-duty antibiotics. On the third day, after no improvement, they discovered that his intestines had perforated, and he needed emergency surgery. Nine days later, Bill emerged from the hospital with a twelve-inch scar, forty pounds lighter and a need to buy new clothes (the silver lining).

Now a typical family story would end there, but nothing that simple for the Foxes. While Bill was recovering in the hospital, we got a call from a teenage boy who wanted to know if we had a small white dog that likes to lick. Well our dear little Tobi escaped from the house and got himself hit by a car, shattering his pelvis, but apparently his togue still worked and he used it to thank his rescuers. He was whisked off to Tufts Veterinary hospital for emergency surgery while Bill recovered in— yes, you guessed it— Tufts Medical Center. Maru, always the finance manager, inquired about a volume discount or at least a frequent user program. No such luck.

The two patients convalesced at home together, licking their wounds, (one literally) and Maru gained much sympathy from the neighbors when she took the two of them for a walk; a hunched over graying man holding his belly and a three legged dog. It was a pathetic sight. The neighbors patted her hand and brought over casseroles for a month. To this day when Maru does not feel like cooking, she puts Tobi in a sling, puts Bill in a robe and takes them for a walk. By the time she gets around the block, a full course meal is waiting for us on the table.

Billy continues to enjoy hockey and has added skateboarding to his repertoire. Skateboarding is intimidating—not the action, but the people, not the kids, the other parents. The first time we went to the indoor skateboard park, Bill and Maru both felt completely out of place and actually frightened. The spectators were tattooed, muscle bound, bandana wearing—and these were the moms. Skateboarding also has its own language. Each sentence always starts with the word "like," ends with "man," and must include the phrases "cool" or "awesome." Here is a typical sentence: "Like I dropped into the bowl, it was awesome, dude and the way my trucks held the rim was like way cool man!" Translation: "I went down the hill and didn't fall."

Ali has adjusted well to sixth grade. She loves to write and is producing her own film, so she is putting all her natural theatrics to productive use. She gave up on horses (too hot in the summer, too cold in the winter, too many flies in the spring, too busy with new friends in the fall (remember, the operative word is "drama"). She went to sleep away camp this summer for two weeks and she loved it. The girls she bunked with became her "sisters" and she already longs for next summer so she can go back—so do we (who said that?). She came back to a renewed sense of self, better appreciation for her brother and twenty pounds of laundry.

Maru had a great year. Her little sister married a great guy she met on the internet (got engaged before she met him, met him, and stayed engaged). Maru wanted to look dazzling at the wedding, so she lost weight using Jenny Craig. The first time she opened the package we marveled at the cute appetizer before realizing it was the entire dinner. She celebrated her weight loss in ridiculous Fox fashion by throwing herself a "Zumba" dance party at a local gym. Just to confirm how frequently a mom throws herself a party, the manager kept asking how old the child is. Maru told them forty-six. He kept wanting to know four or six? He finally got it when she asked if they could do tequila shots. Fifteen middle aged aerobic dancing women wearing boas and sweatpants—how is that for midlife crisis? Bill is going to buy a motorcycle instead.

2007 was another year of many blessings and we have much to be thankful for.

To all our dear friends we wish you God's blessings for a happy holiday season and a peaceful and prosperous 2008!

Bill, Maru, Ali, and Billy

Another Interesting Year

CHRISTMAS 2008

To All Our Friends,
It was another interesting year for the Fox family full of good friends, travels, home improvements, new adventures, and hospital visits (shocker!).

It was almost an upset on the hospitalization front this year. Billy was rushed to the emergency room in November with what was thought to be appendicitis, following four days home with excruciating abdominal pain and three visits to the doctor. They were prepping him for surgery when the X-rays confirmed the true diagnosis. That's right, we have medical evidence that Billy is full of $#%&! Several scoops of a powder laxative, a good large roll of toilet paper and he was as good as new (matches are still off limits).

That left Bill a champ with what was a relatively shallow victory, a measly broken ankle. He fractured it helping Ali's softball team. It did provide some excitement for an otherwise boring Sunday afternoon in Medfield: eleven screaming and crying eleven-year-old girls comforting themselves through the tragedy (they really enjoy getting off on any drama). Police, fire, ambulance on the scene—our tax dollars at work. Bill decided to make the best of the ambulance ride. When asked for a brief medical history, Bill told the EMT in the interest of time, he would stick to the life threatening events and asked him if he wanted them sorted chronologically, by country, alphabetically, or by degree of severity. When they arrived at the hospital, they put Bill ahead of the line; he had finally reached hospital "Platinum Status."

Bill and Maru packed Ali and Billy off to sleep away camp this past summer for two weeks, distinct boy and girl camps. It was an absolute wonderful experience. They slept under star filled nights, strolled around nature, played sports all day long, ate great food and committed to doing it again next year. The kids had a great time too, well, at least Ali did. We are not so sure about Billy. Ali has already made plans to go back. Her many notes home were filled with the joy of being there. Billy's one note home said, "Having a good time, the food is great, I am making friends, when are you picking me up?" We are disregarding the last sentence and packing him off so that we (oops, we mean he) has another fun filled time next year.

Ali continues to be dramatic, but she is finally channeling it to great good (at times). The middle school sponsors a lip sync contest every year and two plays. She won a part in both plays and prizes at the last two lip sync contests with her friend, Rachael. Her jazz choir also won the Northeast Championship this past year. And she was in a local furniture commercial—her two seconds of fame— "That's Nice."

Bill and Billy took up golf this year. They tore up the course, literally. They learned to hit out of bunkers, out of the woods, off the banks of streams and proper placement on the greens. Well, usually they had to hit the ball out of the woods and then often into the bunkers then into a stream and eventually onto a green and occasionally onto the right green (does that count?).

We went on our annual pilgrimage to the White Mountains in New Hampshire this fall to enjoy the foliage. It always serves to remind us that Mother Nature is truly the world's best artist. However, we had an unusual incident at the hotel—yes, unusual even for us.

We brought our dog, Tobi, and set up the back of the van for him to sleep (yes, in a very comfortable way, honestly). Well, the hotel manager noticed him as we were checking in and told us that it was the hotel policy that no dogs could sleep in their parking lot. However, miraculously she knew of someone who could care for Tobi and she just happened to be working that evening. Having no choice, we agreed, and she went to get the dog sitter.

Moments later, the same woman came out front (now with her hair in a ponytail) and said that the manager had told her we had a dog that needed caring for the night. Maru and Bill looked at each other and with jaws dropped Maru asked, "Didn't we just speak to you?" With a puzzled look she shook her head no, then told us if we were interested in the dog sitting, we could meet her out front in fifteen minutes. Moments later the manager came out (no ponytail) and asked if we were all set with the dog sitter. We hesitantly said, yes. Bill asked her if she had a twin and she shook her head no. Our hands (and tongues) tied we let Tobi stay with Sybil. "They" delivered him back to us safe and sound the next day. We said good-bye to "them" and were on our way. As we pulled out, we noticed a car with a beautiful Golden Retriever pulling in. We considered warning them but figured why spoil their Christmas letter.

2008 was another year of many blessings and we have much to be thankful for.

To all our dear friends we wish you God's blessings for a happy holiday season and a peaceful and (hopefully) prosperous 2009!

Bill, Maru, Ali, and Billy

2008

Another Interesting Year

CHRISTMAS 2009

To All Our Friends,
It was another interesting year for the Fox family full of good friends, travels new adventures and yes, hospital visits.

We rang in the New Year with our first (and perhaps our last) family New Year's Eve Party. We hosted a neighborhood potluck party, and we are still cleaning up after it (seriously). Maru decided it would be fun to give the kids bags of foil confetti and then a fabulously fun confetti fight ensued. For a half hour straight, thirty kids armed with their own bag raced around the house throwing confetti at everything. It was in our underwear drawers, in every closet, in the molding, on our toothbrushes (we all looked like we got braces after we brushed our teeth the next morning).

In May, we invited the same group for a Memorial Day BBQ, and as we prepared to welcome our friends, we turned on the ceiling fans and watched mounds of confetti we had not noticed on the blades spread all over the family room. It was Happy New Year all over again; the memory lived on. The neighbors asked about our doing it again this year. We will be in hiding.

Bill, once again, had the most interesting medical experience. He went to the gym by his office, dressed to work out, and brought his office clothes with him. After showering he realized he forgot his underwear, so he put on his pants (sans under garments). A little jing/jangle action, but who would know. He then remembered he had an appointment for a circulation test at the hospital that morning, but as he was told they were only going to attach electrodes to his feet, no worries. He got to the exam room, the doctor came in, handed him a hospital gown, and told him to undress to his underwear. Ok, what to do?

The doctor came in a couple of minutes later and his jaw dropped. Thinking on his feet Bill blurted out, "All my hospital visits and I still do not know how to put these gowns on," as he sat with the gown tied around him like a diaper. The doctor told him his circulation was fine, but suggested he move up his next appointment with the neurologist.

On a more serious medical note, Maru's mom took a very bad fall this winter down some stairs at her home in Mexico City and needed emergency surgery to remove a blood clot in her brain. Always resilient, she defied the odds and is doing much better, but has a long road ahead. Fortunately, she was well enough to dance with her husband of fifty years at a wonderful golden anniversary party attended by two hundred in a beautiful hacienda while her children serenaded them. A Kodak moment.

Ali continued to excel in drama and sometimes even on the stage. She also joined the ranks of the Fox family medical tradition when we found she was allergic to some medications she was taking which caused severe migraines. Generally speaking, if there is a potential for headaches, tremors, hives, or your head spinning off your shoulders, listed as potential side effects of any drug, the Fox family is the 0.1% who gets them. Frankly, we do not know why the ads just don't say, "The Fox family should be aware of the following potential side effects," and save the rest of the population the trouble.

Ali also had a small cavity. Besides the fact that she did not like the color of the procedure room, hated the flavor of the topical Novocain, and tried to bite the technician, they were able to fill the cavity. We were very proud of her.

Summer camp was enjoyed by all this year; however, no matter how much we pleaded, begged, and cajoled, the kids refused to spend more time there. Ali went to the same camp for the third straight year. She loved it, hated it, made new friends, cried each day, laughed each day, didn't want to go, didn't want to leave and didn't want to make a decision—a well-rounded thirteen year old experience. Billy opted for a hockey camp. And while most kids want to be outside swimming, Billy's perfect summer is inside at thirty-two degrees, on ice all day long. When he wasn't on the ice this summer, he was on the golf course and hits a 5-iron better than Bill can hit a drive.

The family summer vacation got off to a rough start. Maru and kids left August 1st at 8 a.m. on a connecting flight to Mexico City and Bill hit the golf course at 8:01. Then the call, "Honey, we are in Houston and we have a problem!" Seems Billy's passport had expired and so the airline shipped the wetbacks back to Boston. It took a week to get Billy's new passport, the same day Bill was to fly to meet them in Mexico to visit Maru's family, so they were able to fly together; Maru was thrilled, Bill's "pre" vacation ruined. While in Mexico,

Another Interesting Year

Maru went to her twenty-fifth college reunion. Forty biochemical engineers and their families in a Mexican resort. Look up "nerds" in Wikipedia and a picture of this reunion pops up, so we fit right in.

Maru has taken up photography and photography has taken over every aspect of our lives. "Bill, hold that pose, the way the light catches your pot belly in your pajamas is perfect." "Billy, be a sweetie and see if you can get that huge player, Number 14, to check you against the boards again, Mommy missed that shot!" We cannot make a move without it being captured on film, our own paparazzi.

2009 was another year of many blessings and we have much to be thankful for and now we have the photos to prove it.

To all our dear friends we wish you God's blessings for a happy and holiday season and a peaceful, prosperous 2010!

Bill, Maru, Ali, and Billy

2009

Another Interesting Year

CHRISTMAS 2010

To All Our Friends,
It was another interesting year for the Fox family full of good friends, travels, new adventures and yes, hospital visits.

It is official. We are horrible parents. Ali was really struggling with her ADHD and her therapist suggested a special camp that is all about focus and teaches the drive to get things done. It all sounded wonderful and perfect for what Ali needed. The camp was in North Carolina and highly sought after so when we got word that there was a place for her, we acted quickly, jumped on a plane to Charlotte, and then took a two hour drive to install Ali at the "camp."

Now under most circumstances, parents usually thoroughly check out a camp and make sure the camp life would be enjoyable, but as everything happened so fast, we took a leap of faith that it was a normal type of camp with ADHD therapy. Our first clue that this was not your conventional camp should have been that all she was to bring were five panties and three bras. The second clue should have been the five minutes they gave us to say good-bye before they told us "bye-bye" in no uncertain terms and they would be in touch in a week. It was when we went to the parent workshop there three weeks later, that we learned the truth.

We were told, since we could not see her, that Ali was adjusting nicely to living in a tent, and to the daily eight mile mountain hikes and that she had finally mastered making fires by smacking a rock with a piece of steel. And while we were dining on Chateaubriand at the Biltmore Estate during our visit, she was eating lentils and rice for the twentieth day in a row.

Her graduation, after week nine, involved her taking care of us in the woods, and she amazed us. She built the fire, cooked us lentils, rice and cheese and put our stuff in a tree where the black bears could not reach it (one attacked her camp the week before). She emerged a new young woman full of confidence, determination, and respect for herself. Maru and Bill were overwhelmed with the change in her.

We were also overwhelmed by how lost one can get when you need to go to the bathroom in the middle of the night in the Black Mountains with no light. Both Maru and Bill wondered off separately into the woods and found each other, and without our glasses we both kind of look like bears; and let's just say that we are very loud when we are scared and Maru can punch hard when she is fighting off what she thinks is a wild animal. And Bill can, let's just say, yell very loud when he is being punched by someone who thinks they are being attacked by a wild animal. Seems we woke up all the other parents. Kids all slept through it including Ali.

The rest of the summer was relatively typical. Billy went to hockey sleep away camp, golf camp and day camp for two weeks each. We also took in a Red Sox game one beautiful summer evening. While we were heading to the parking lot, Bill was trying to keep up with Billy and Maru fell a few paces behind. When Maru caught up to Bill, she found him speaking to an incredibly good-looking guy that she seemed to know, so she assumed he was a co-worker of Bill's that she met at a function. Bill called Maru over in Spanish. The guy, noticing this, kindly addressed her in Spanish. She gave him a big hug and the two new friends started to walk down the street together arm and arm; Bill and the guy's wife were left to walk behind them as the two chatted away in Spanish. We all bid farewell and Maru gave the man another big hug and a kiss and said she hoped to see both him and his wife again soon. Maru told Bill that we should absolutely invite this nice couple to our next holiday party. Bill said he would check and see if her new best friend, Senator Scott Brown, was available that night.

On the hospital visit front, Bill did not disappoint. In October, just when we thought we were in the clear, he was cleaning the pool before it was closed for the season, slipped on some acorns, fell, bounced off the cement, landed in the pool and cracked three ribs. He managed to get out of the pool on his own, but since he could not bend over and get into the car, Maru had to call an ambulance. The dispatcher told Maru, "Not a problem Mrs. Fox, and yes of course we know the address."

Maru and the paramedics shared greetings and got caught up when they arrived. Bill mentioned he was in a lot of pain, so they finally loaded him in. A new member of the paramedic team was riding with the group and explained to Maru to not worry, stay calm and do not speed to the hospital. Maru, ever so experienced, but good natured, humored the guy and listened intently, even managed to call up a tear for effect. Then once the ambulance pulled out of the driveway, she set about her normal day and put a wash in the machine, walked the dog, paid some bills online, wrote a poem about the incident, prepared dinner for the week and put it in the freezer and then headed to the hospital. It is nice to know she has her priorities straight.

    The kids are doing well. Billy is adjusting nicely to middle school and Ali is in her freshman year of high school. Ali, always creative, got the lead in the school musical *Chicago* and was awesome as Roxy Hart. Billy tried his hand at the stage this year and performed along with two friends in the middle school lip sync contest. Ali was a regular lip sync performer and won prizes two years in a row. She and her friends devoted themselves to perfectly choreographed performances. They literally practiced every day for one whole month before the show. Billy and his friends practiced every minute for one hour before the show.

    Maru and Bill hid towards the back of the auditorium, terrified of what might happen on stage given all the "prep" work. The curtains opened, and they rocked, syncing to Motley Crue's *Home Sweet Home*. Bill and Maru suddenly sat up in the seats. Members of the audience took out the cell phones, loaded the flame and waved them in the air; and some of their kids did too. A group of sixth grade girls behind Bill and Maru started to scream, "We love you, Billy!" Maru turned around and screamed, "Seriously?" They won a prize; go figure.

2010

2010 was another year of many blessings and we have much to be thankful for. We hope you are all happy and well.

To all our dear friends, we wish you God's blessings for a happy holiday season and a peaceful, prosperous 2011!

Bill, Maru, Ali, and Billy

Another Interesting Year

CHRISTMAS 2011

To All Our Friends,
It has been another interesting year for the Fox family full of travels, adventures, milestones, and crime sprees.

Bill turned fifty and Maru threw him a surprise party. Lots of people came. They ate, they drank, they danced, and they left. Maru turned fifty and Bill took Maru on a wonderful exotic trip to Turkey that included hot air balloon rides, romantic Champaign breakfasts in beautiful fields, boat rides up the Bosporus River, and Swirling Dervish dances. Bill's party was in a beer hall.

Most people hit their fifties and celebrate their mid-life crisis by doing something out of character, like buy a Harley, and some actually learn how to ride the Harley they bought. Bill and Maru stole a piano. They stole it from Ali's boarding school as they were picking her up from her last day of class. It was kind of an accidental theft, but the authorities called it a theft, nevertheless.

Ali's voice teacher said there was a keyboard they could have for her. So naturally they thought that the upright piano in the school's common room that had a vase of flowers and a sign across it that said, "Congratulations class of 2011," was the keyboard she was referring to. They carefully dismantled it using the toolbox they stole from the janitor's closet and loaded it into their van. As they were about to make their getaway, the music teacher drove up and, well, caught them.

They spent the next two hours re-assembling the piano under the watchful eye of her not so amused husband. By the way, no one in the family even plays the piano.

Once again, we did some construction on the house and we hired a contractor that was excellent, but all the workers had ADD. They would start something, get bored and start something else, get bored and kept going at it this way for twelve weeks, nothing done, but everything in progress. If they were in a bathroom and decided it was time to work on the kitchen, they would simply leave the bathroom, move to the kitchen, put a drop cloth over the stove, never mind food was cooking, and paint. If you were sleeping in a room they wanted to work in, a drop cloth went over you and they painted. It went on like this until one day they put lids on the paint cans in each room and left. The house went from utter chaos to complete, overnight.

It is official: Maru is a menace on the road. Thirty years of driving and never as much as a parking ticket. This year she has gotten four tickets. We thought her previous spotless record was due to careful driving, but it was actually sheer luck. She was shocked to discover that route numbers were not equivalent to the speed limit. People would honk and tailgate her when she drove 27 MPH on Rt. 27 and dove to the side of the road as she dragged raced down Rt. 109. Just imagine the chaos she caused on Rt. 495.

The big family vacation this year was a cruise that Bill's mother treated the whole family to. Thanks, Mom! One night, Bill and Maru were sent to reserve seats for the comedy show.

2011

Before the comedians took the stage, they were hosting an "adult" game night, kind of a "we dare you" contest with judges. Bill and Maru idiotically got swept up in the action and after five rounds of doing one more ridiculous thing after another, they were in third place out of twenty teams; and when the emcee asked if anyone would do a jump split for points, Maru could not help herself and performed a beautiful, flying split to thunderous applause. At first, Bill mistook the look on Maru's face as ecstasy. It was actually agony as she tore a muscle. So, as they entered the final round now tied for first place, Bill's mom, who was the only one that had arrived so far, replaced Maru. They still had a chance to take it all, but she refused to take off her bra under her sweater—spoil sport!

Ali turned fifteen and celebrated her quinceañera in Disney World with two friends, her Aunt Rocio, and her mom, and had a fabulous time. She also started a new school this year called Chapel Hill-Chauncey Hall and she loves it. She has made a ton of new friends and is very happy. The school has a creative flare to it, which is right up Ali's alley. She is very active in the drama club and was recently cast as the stepmother in the upcoming musical version of *Cinderella*.

Billy became a teenager this year and is doing great. He is still all about hockey which means the entire family is all about hockey and even our vacations are all about hockey. Who the hell goes to Minnesota on vacation? Hockey kids and their crazy parents and their not so amused sisters, that's who! By the way, we are heading to Toronto for a Christmas hockey tournament. Fortunately, we really like his team and their families and Ali is bringing a friend, so all is well. It will be a nice way to spend the holidays.

To all our dear friends, we wish you God's blessings for a happy healthy holiday season and a peaceful and prosperous 2012!

Bill, Maru, Ali, and Billy

2011

Another Interesting Year

CHRISTMAS 2012

To All Our Friends,

It has been another interesting year for the Fox family full of travels, adventures and yes, hospital visits.

At the time of this writing, the Fox family is happy to report that the only ER visit this year was for Bill (naturally). It was for a set of stitches in the center of his tongue, a first even for him. But what he lacked in substance, he made up in style. Maru and Bill were at a formal benefit for Children's Hospital and it seems that there was a chicken bone mixed in with the sauce, and of course of the 500 dinners, it landed on Bill's plate and of course he chomped down on it.

Normally one would say something to their spouse when there is enough blood to soak several napkins, but they were playing salsa music and Maru wanted to salsa. So, Bill (the wonderful, kind, and caring husband he is) hid the little problem and stole the napkins off the table, one by one, to soak up the blood when no one was looking. He finally ran out of napkins to steal and Maru noticed the blood spilling out of the sides of his mouth. Normally, that would cause most spouses to scream, but she simply said, "Too bad this is not a Halloween Ball, you look like a vampire."

While she debated in her head about leaving salsa, Maru (the wonderful, sensible, caring wife that she is) suggested they head to the ER before Bill lost another pint of blood. In tux and ball gown, they made quite the entrance at 2 a.m.

amongst the drunks and knife victims. It was the first time in their lives they were referred to as the best dressed people in the place. It is a moment they will cherish always.

This was a significant travel year for the Fox family. We ended 2011 with a hockey tournament in Toronto, our first international hockey trip, and had a blast. Ali brought her friend, Sienna, so that she had someone to hang with, Billy had sixteen of his friends with him, and Bill and Maru had the hockey parents, one of whom (a policeman) smuggled four hundred Jell-O shots across the border, so the little we remember about the tournament was great. We heard something about our team losing. If that is true, it is a shame.

While Toronto was great, the big family vacation this year was a wonderful trip to Europe. Well, Bill, Maru, and Ali felt it was wonderful. Billy tolerated it, barely (no golf, no hockey and foreign food). We hit Paris, Venice, Florence, and Rome. The weather was crazy. It rained most of the time we were in Paris, but regardless, we took it all in and even toured the city on Segway— a little National Lampoon action with the Fox family careening down the sidewalks as unsuspecting Parisian's dove to the side.

Another adventure was going to the top of the Eiffel Tower. The line for the elevator was three hours long so the kids convinced us to walk up the stairs. It was crazy, but a blast. People in different languages alternated words of encouragement as the insane tourists, big and small, climbed as a team. And while it was tough, it was worth it, and the video of our ascent captures the beauty that is Paris and the fun we had despite the pain.

Italy on the other hand, was sunny and one hundred plus degrees every day. Venice was by far the family favorite, gelato and gondolas, a perfect combination. Rome was a trip down memory lane for Maru, as she was a high school exchange student there. We also got to experience the World Cup finals between Italy and Spain in an outdoor restaurant. Got a little bit scary when Italy lost and about one thousand rowdy Spanish tourists started to march in triumph. We tried to blend in by speaking Spanish, but our I Love Italy tee-shirts (in English) kind of gave us away.

We have another student in the house! Maru decided to go back to school and is taking online certificate courses from the University of Pennsylvania in that very useful topic of Greek mythology. So, every night she is sitting in the bedroom with headphones on and an iPad in her lap studying and arguing with the screen. After each lesson, the students take an on-line test; to pass and move on you need to score 16/20. That is not good enough for Maru. If she gets less than a 19, she re-takes the test, staying up till all hours determined to get a 19. Once she got an 18 and spent two days proving the professor was wrong with the other students in the class (all 50,000 of them) cheering her on, mostly because many of them needed that damn question correct to make a 16.

Well, she was correct (of course), and while the class thought she was awesome, our fire department not so much. Fire trucks were called to the house as Billy caused a small grease fire trying to make bacon since Maru got so caught up

Another Interesting Year

in the challenge, she forgot to make dinner.

Ali turned sixteen and has her learner's permit and is turning out to be a very good driver. She is in her junior year and is mapping out all the universities that have drama departments for site visits this year. She remains highly active in theater. Last year, she was the lead in the musical version of Cinderella after the lead had to drop out, and she was magnificent. Eight songs, numerous costumes changes, she lit up the stage. By the second night word got out it was great, and she performed to a standing room only crowd. We were immensely proud!

Billy is fourteen and is doing great. In addition to hockey, his new obsession is golf. Talk about a dichotomy of passions. On the golf course he is gentile and considered. Phrases like "nice shot" and "I believe you putt first" that flowed from his lips in the summer became, "If I get the chance, I will rip the head off their #9 #$%@" during the fall hockey season. We are thrilled as we believe this is what the shrinks call a well-balanced child; thus, validation of our parenting skills.

To all our dear friends, we wish you God's blessings for a happy holiday season and a peaceful and prosperous 2013!

Bill, Maru, Ali, and Billy

2012

Another Interesting Year

CHRISTMAS 2013

To All Our Friends,
It has been yet another interesting year for the Fox family full of the usual travels, adventures with a few relatively boring hospital visits thrown in.

Ali is a high school senior and the Fox family was introduced to the art of evaluating colleges. Most college bound seniors evaluate schools by their programs. But our Ali is focused squarely on one thing: location, location, location. (Perhaps she will be a realtor when she grows up). She wants to go someplace warm, close to a beach, near a city, but with a suburban campus. They have to have a slant to the arts and a large international student body. The food needs to be restaurant quality and there must be plenty of closet space in the dorm room. We have identified two such places on the planet, so we are keeping our fingers crossed.

For years she has told us that she wanted to major in musical theater, but in October she had an epiphany. She came to the conclusion that for every role she would vie for there would be another two hundred others going for it as well. Instead, she was going to major in film production so that she can actually be independent and make a living. You may recall that day in October. It is the one when the ground around you suddenly started to rock; that day that flocks of birds heading south suddenly lost their way; it is the day our daughter's frontal lobe started to close and the heavens took note. Alleluia!!

The hospital visit stories are indeed incredibly boring this year. Yes, we had a few, Bill actually had nine, but they didn't even require an overnight stay, so they are barely worth mentioning. The only mildly amusing one was his spinal tap.

We are frequent fliers at Tufts Medical Center, and they have performed miracles for Bill, but there are pitfalls of teaching hospitals. There he was naked and strapped to a table in a room that was barely fifty degrees, face down, bent over like the letter "r" and in a head harness that kept his mouth shut, when a doctor walked in and in a voice that sounded like a boy going through puberty, announced that this was the first time he was doing "a tap." Then the nurse had to remind him to use the 10 cm needle instead of the 5 cm he had in his hand and then he proceeded unsuccessfully seven times to get the needle in, each time announcing "damn, bone again! Sorry Mr. Fox, this is my first-time doing this," like that was supposed to make it okay.

Bill couldn't yell, but after the seventh attempt he managed to get his hand free and grabbed the doctor by the belt strap and pulled him close enough to say through the head harness, that if he did not get a real doctor in here to do this Bill would hunt him down and jam the 10 cm needle into his eye when this was all over. His "mentor" arrived five minutes later (clearly paged due to Bill's rage) and got the needle in on the first try. Doogie Houser managed to escape before Bill got a good look at him. Wimp!

Billy is a high school freshman, still plays hockey, but

has become obsessed with golf. He averaged 36 holes a day during the summer and had some 72-hole days and has a low single digit handicap. When he is not playing golf, he is practicing; and when he is not practicing, he is watching the Golf Channel; and when he is not doing that, he is at the golf store testing new equipment. He has become the mayor of the golf club. Want a good tee time and they are all booked? Call and say you are with Billy. Need a line of credit at the club restaurant? Tell them you are with Billy. No need to mention Bill, he has to say he is with Billy when he wants a good tee time too.

Maru is doing great. She continues to take online courses from all the Ivy League schools and continues to get almost perfect grades, but we are sorry to report that she is no closer to a degree than when she started. Instead of stringing a bunch of useless courses on one topic together, Maru takes "interesting" classes, so while she has a base understanding of everything from sociology to zoology, she has not gained a base understanding of what it takes to get a damn graduate degree!

Bill finally had his midlife crisis...at least Maru hopes so. Bill has always been a relatively practical shopper, especially on big ticket items, so when it came time to buy a new car and pass his nine-year-old Acura to Ali, Maru expected another basic foreign sedan. Instead, he drove home in an Audi A5 convertible. It is totally impractical, fits practically nothing and two weeks after he got it a truck smashed into it putting his baby in the shop for the entire convertible season. Bill cannot even enjoy a normal impractical midlife crisis.

Another Interesting Year

Christmas is a time of reflection for most of us and we are no different. Overall, we have a great deal to be thankful for. We have been in the Boston area almost ten years and while we have been incredibly happy and have made some wonderful friends, somehow, we still hung onto the notion that we were New Yorkers. It is where we bought our first house, where we became parents, where our kids started school. However, 2013 was very different.

The Marathon bombings put this in motion. Watching how the city sprang into action and how the rest of the country had our back had great impact. Then the day of the capture we were awoken by a call from Ali's school that it was on lockdown as her school was right on the Watertown border where the bastards were suspected of being. Nerve wracking day to say the least and then it was over, one dead, one captured and Bill and Maru became proud Bostonians.

To all our dear friends, we wish you God's blessings for a happy holiday season and a peaceful and prosperous 2014.

Bill, Maru, Ali, and Billy

2013

Another Interesting Year

CHRISTMAS 2014

To All Our Friends,

It has been another interesting year for the Fox family full of the usual travels, adventures and of course, a few hospital visits.

Maru decided to join the ranks of the employed! After being a stay at home mom for the past eighteen years, with Ali in college and Billy as a sophomore in high school, she decided that now was the time. It was important to her that she use the degree she worked long and hard for, bio-chemical engineering. Fortunately, an opportunity came her way at Tufts Medical Center. They were so excited to have her that they agreed to wait until after the holidays. The role involves the study of large dose intake of vitamins in the body. Actually, the job involves the study of large doses of Vitamin D in her body; yes, Maru is a lab rat. They told her that she is representing the Latin population and she is honored and humbled by the responsibility.

Bill continues to happily work at his company. His golf swing hasn't improved, his 5K running time has not decreased, and he took his usual ride to the hospital in the back of an ambulance this year. Yep, status quo on the Bill front. He was sitting at a conference room table on one of those captain's chairs leading his staff meeting and mid-sentence he just disappeared (as the others in the room later recounted). His chair snapped in half and he fell back headfirst onto a concrete floor with a thin layer of carpet. A whirlwind of activity followed with security and then the paramedics. They asked him how he felt, and he told them he had head pains, nausea, dizziness, "The typical way I feel at the office." Nevertheless, they decided he needed to be checked out.

It was all one big crazy scene of commotion with people saying someone should call Maru and others saying don't call Maru since she will think he's unconscious, or worse if he is not the one doing the calling. Well someone caved and called Maru and sure enough she thought he was near death because, "Why isn't he calling if he is ok?" (Lesson here for the rest of you!).

The commotion continued until the paramedics asked what hospital to take him to and his entire team screamed in harmony "Tufts," Bill's well-known home away from home. When they wheeled Bill in, it was like a family reunion. Nurses and ER workers who recognized him came over to say hello, like regulars at a local pub. Given Bill's history they scanned him head to toe, found a lot of things wrong—even a few related to the fall including a concussion.

Ali had an amazing year. She won the lead again in her high school musical playing Belle in *Beauty and the Beast* to rave reviews. She actually graduated high school (touch and go for a while) and she got into the school of her choice, Lynn University in Boca Raton. The adjustment to college life has been tough for her since the routine is so boring. She wakes up, goes to a class, then goes to the pool, then to another class, then goes to the beach, and then goes to dinner before doing her homework by the pool, which of course has Wi-Fi and a swim up bar.

Essentially, we are paying for a country club for young adults that she says has a well-stocked library, although under cross-examination she has trouble pointing out exactly where it is. She recently won the lead in the musical as a freshman which shocked her and a few senior drama majors even more. The school will be sending the theater group to perform the show called *Is There Life After High School?* to Dublin, Ireland this spring. And yes, there is life after high school for Ali and it is going quite well.

Billy's life continues to revolve around golf. His game improved dramatically this year; he has a very low handicap and made varsity as a sophomore in a Division 1 school. And in a year that was meant to be a "build year" for the team, he and his teammates went on to win the Mass State Championship for Xaverian Brothers H.S. It has been an awesome golf year! Well done, Billy. At the season's end and before the temperature dipped below forty degrees, Bill and Billy enjoyed their last round and in one of the father-son moments, Bill told Billy how much he enjoys playing with him on the weekends and Billy, very tenderly responded, "Thanks Dad, but the truth is I walk all week around the course and playing with you simply allows me to ride in a cart." So much for that Hallmark card moment!

As many of you are aware, Maru lost her beloved mother this past spring. She was a wonderful woman, adored by all and she left the world a better place by just being in it. We all

Another Interesting Year

miss her terribly, but grateful that we had her in our lives.

Maru has since gone to Mexico every other month to check in on her dad who has been in failing health which has only gotten much worse since the passing of his wife. It was on one of those trips this past summer that Maru scared the hell out of Bill. She does not think she did anything wrong. We will let you decide.

Bill woke up unusually late on a Sunday and noticed that he had an e-mail from Maru. It simply read: "After a peaceful night, the first in many, my dad left early this morning with Jesus." Bill started to book flights, cancelled his meetings for the next day, and finally reached Maru expecting to find her in hysterics, only to find her calm and cool. Bill, thinking she is in shock, told her how sorry he was and that they would get down there as soon as they could. "What are you talking about?" she asked. "But your dad!" answered Bill. "Oh yeah, isn't it wonderful? Dad felt so good he went out early this morning for breakfast with the driver, Jesus." Okay, we will leave it to you, did Bill overreact? He thinks not.

To all our friends, we wish you God's blessings for a happy holiday season and a peaceful and prosperous 2015!

Bill, Maru, Ali, and Billy

2014

Another Interesting Year

CHRISTMAS 2015

To All Our Friends,
Okay, let's cut to the chase. With the exception of Ali, overall, the year basically sucked for the rest of us. Here is our sad Christmas letter. We did our best to highlight some of the bright spots in addition to the drama.

Maru lost her beloved dad in February, and because of all the damned blizzards we kept having in the Boston area, we couldn't even get to the funeral in time.

And while we often weave what has become the annual Bill hospital story into the mix, this year he outdid himself. And for someone who has had a brain tumor, it was an incredible feat. Maru had become immune to his lack of immunities, but this time he even scared the hell out of her which we thought was impossible.

Bill contracted sepsis as a result of a botched routine outpatient medical procedure. Maru knew he was in trouble when the ER nurse asked if Bill had a health proxy on file while seven doctors rushed him into the ICU. He spent the night delirious with fever while his kidneys and liver started to shut down, but after two days the infection started to respond to antibiotics. He was on IV for three weeks and then the infection made a brief reoccurrence (remember we are talking Bill), but in the end, just another routine near death experience for Bill Fox. Once again, we count our blessings and our very good health insurance.

Another Interesting Year

    Billy spent the summer playing golf and most of the rest of the year watching it. He placed well in several high-level tournaments and seemed to be doing great until the end of the summer when he fell into a funk. And in the Fox family, when a teenager falls into a funk they wake up and find themselves in a wilderness program, wearing a backpack, fending off wildlife and cooking rice and beans over a fire they built with sticks and rocks. He is back, de-funked and doing great!

    On another trip that Maru, Bill, and Billy took to check some boarding schools in North Carolina, we almost died. We were on the highway when it began to rain and then the rain turned to a torrential downpour. In the meantime, Maru was on the phone with Ali when her phone started buzzing loudly. She was so mad at the interruption, since it is a rare occurrence when our teenagers actually call instead of text, she discarded the message. Then Bill's phone started to buzz so Maru promptly turned it off too so she could hear the rare call from Ali. Then hail the size of golf balls started to rain down on them and it got so dark we could not see. Bill barely saw an exit and headed off the highway.

    Finally, the skies cleared, and we saw uprooted trees and overturned cars all around us, and then all of a sudden the blare of sirens seemed to come from everywhere. Turned out that the message Maru ignored was an emergency alert to take cover immediately due to a tornado in our immediate vicinity. Oh, and the reason we almost died was a debate over the perfect shade of pink for Ali's pedicure.

    On a more upbeat note, Bill and Maru made the news.

2015

Maru had the wild idea that they should take advantage of our first empty nester Halloween (Ali being in college and Billy fending off wild boars in Utah) and go to Salem, Massachusetts (yes, of burning witches at the stake fame). Bill suggested it might not be a good idea. He had seen news reports of people getting shot and friends who live in the area leave town for Halloween week to escape the lunatics, drunks and street thugs who consider Salem their sanctuary on Halloween. And let's face it, our luck this year had been bad even for us.

Maru dismissed the reports calling the locals "wimps!" So she whipped up impressive costumes using nothing but our own clothes, which is a sad commentary on our wardrobe, and off we went to Salem as "Catrinos"—think Mexican Day of the Dead and if you don't know what that is think skeletons dressed in semi-formal attire.

Salem did not disappoint; it was insane, so we fit right in. We were a big hit and paraded and posed for pictures for two hours until about 9 p.m. when the real crazies started coming out. At that point we smartly decided that we would leave before the riots got into full swing.

On our way home, we were hungry, so we stopped at Friendly's family restaurant. You would have thought no one ever sat in a restaurant in full skeleton costumes in dresses and a tux with the way they all just stared at us. Really, people can be so rude.

Well, the next day we turned on the morning news and we were the featured Salem crazies! We dress up like dead people and we are a news story. Our fifteen seconds of fame can be found on YouTube https://youtu.be/j3QyJSFc2ME. We are quite the sensation with over 800 views, and we have not viewed it more than 750 times!

Ali has had another amazing year on the performing front. She was cast in the lead of her college musical, *Is There Life After High School* which met with strong reviews. Consequently, the troop was sent to Ireland to perform for a week which was very exciting for her. Quoting Ali, "People are actually paying to see me perform!" Her performance caught the eye of a record producer and he recorded five songs with her that they co-wrote together over the summer. Her first single is meant to be released at the end of January. Not sure where it will all go, but hell, we think it is cool. The only people who have recorded her thus far are Bill and Maru with an iPhone from the audience, so it is already a huge step up.

We did have a really good high note to the year which was our wonderful family trip to England this summer. We truly had a great time, well Bill and Maru did. The kids did too for a few days, especially when the car we rented caught fire and the British Bobbies had to rescue us. But then the kids got bored and flew back early so Bill and Maru did what any good parents would do, they extended their trip and went to Iceland! Then the real fun began. What an amazing time and it was awesome. Did we mention the kids were not with us? It was really, really awesome!!

To all our dear friends, we wish you God's blessings for a

happy healthy holiday season and a peaceful and prosperous 2016!

Bill, Maru, Ali, and Billy

Another Interesting Year

CHRISTMAS 2016

To All Our Friends,

It has been another interesting year for the Fox family full of travel, transitions, trauma, quarantine, and visits to the hospital. We are therefore happy to report it was a relatively normal year for us.

This year's patient of the year was Tobi. Yes, Tobi our eleven-pound ball of fur took top honors. Tobi was attacked by a vicious dog and got several deep puncture wounds, and just when he had recovered, he got attacked by a coyote. Tobi was out in our front yard doing his before bed business when Bill heard a loud yelp. He ran to check out what was going on when Tobi collapsed in front of him in a pool of blood. Maru came running due to all the commotion and she scooped him up as Bill got the car. Tobi was still in attack mode, so he bit Maru twice as she tried to comfort him.

They rushed him to a nearby 24-hour vet clinic, and they stabilized him, but he needed help breathing. So, they equipped Maru with a breathing pump to use on him and they sent us to Tufts Veterinary Hospital. The hospital was about forty five minutes away, but the band *Cold Play* was performing at nearby Gillette Stadium and the roads were blocked, so Bill had to drive like a mad man around cars full of middle aged groupies drunk on too much chardonnay. They got there an hour later, and they rushed Tobi into emergency surgery. The damn coyote completely crushed his rib cage and consequently our savings account. Four days of intensive care and he made a full recovery; our savings account is still on the mend; and Cold Play is now banned from the house.

The night of the attack, Maru's hand was so swollen from Tobi's bite that the vet told us that we needed to take Maru to the ER to have her checked for an infection. It took four hours to be seen and to get a tetanus shot.

Well the next day, the police came and had orders to put our pet "Maru" in quarantine for possible rabies from being bit by a fox. Maru explained that she was Maru Fox who was bit by Tobi who was bit by a coyote, and he was recovering at the veterinary hospital. As you can imagine, this went in circles for quite a while.

Police: "What's a Maru?"

Maru: "I am Maru. It is short for Maria Eugenia."

Police: "Why is your son Tobi at the vet?"

Maru: "Tobi is our dog, he is at the vet, our son is named Billy and he is in the wilderness."

Police: "So was Billy bit by the Fox?"

Maru: "No, our dog Tobi was bit by a coyote."

Police: "How many foxes live on your property?"

Maru: "Currently three, but when Billy gets home, that will make four.

Police:" Mam, just don't let Maru, Tobi or Billy near other animals for six weeks."

Maru promised.

Billy spent most of the year in Utah at a boarding school, and after some initial adjustment he had an awesome experience. Bill and Maru went on monthly visits. One of those visits coincided with a parent's weekend and there was a notice encouraging parents to join their sons for a "leisurely" triathlon race. The teachers and coaches were very interested in parent participation and so were actively recruiting participants and you guessed it, Bill signed up to compete with Billy.

Bill is not in the best of shape but has run a couple of marathons in his life and he runs about three miles most days, so he was not totally unprepared mentally to be destroyed physically. They said it was a "leisurely" triathlon and as all the parents of all ages, shapes and sizes had signed up he figured "what the hell."

The morning of the event arrived and so did three hundred of the fittest people in Salt Lake City…and Bill and the other out of shape parents. Then one of the parents asked Bill which event he was participating in? "What do you mean, which event, isn't this a triathlon?"

The other unfit parents laughed and said, "Well yes, technically, but didn't you know that you could sign up for an individual event?"

That was the all-important "leisurely" part Bill missed. At that moment they announced the names of the school parents who were participating in the full triathlon. (Bill and two other suckers); no turning back. The whistle blew and the torture began. Bill finished his first and last triathlon (5K run, 20K bike ride, 1K swim) not in last place (his goal). Billy finished and looked like he just took a lap around the park, damn youth!

Another Interesting Year

Ali had another amazing year on the performing front. Her debut album Free launched on all the major music sites in April and her featured single, also called Free, hit #23 on the Billboard charts this summer. Thousands of downloads, hit #7 in parts of Eastern Europe (guess anything with the word "free" still becomes an anthem there) and at fractions of a penny for each play, she earned almost enough money to pay for her trip to Indianapolis to visit her friends for New Year's! She learned firsthand why most performers, even the so-called successful ones, are also professional waitstaff.

On the very exciting side, she was invited to the Grammys as an "up and comer" and she honored her dad by inviting him to be her escort. Ali got invited to a couple of pre-parties, saw Adele in rehearsals and Bill went to the bathroom with Ed Sheeran (sounds really creepy on paper but exciting in real life). The live show was the best event either of them had ever been to and they were treated to fabulous seats.

Ali is living in New York City now, trying to make it in musical theater and getting adjusted to the ultra-competitive world of performing. She is going back to school part time in January to secure a plan B in production while continuing to audition for everything and anything. She did get a couple of bit parts in commercials and the HBO series Ballers and performed in a couple of cabarets, so she is making some headway and literally living the dream, a heavily subsidized dream!

To all our dear friends, we wish you God's blessings for a happy holiday season and a peaceful and prosperous 2017.

Bill, Maru, Ali, and Billy

2016

Another Interesting Year

CHRISTMAS 2017

To All Our Friends,
For those of you who gather around and enjoy the trials and tribulations of the Fox Family as part of your Christmas tradition, this year's letter is going to suck. Simply put, we don't got much. Tobi had another crappy year, but for the rest of us, it was pretty good. Sorry!

Bill took advantage of an early retirement package offer this past summer. He expects to go back to work eventually, well probably, okay maybe, but he is not in a rush. He is thoroughly enjoying himself and when the right job comes along, he will take the plunge, hopefully before they run out of money. In the meantime, Bill and Maru have fallen into a boring routine. Up each morning around 8 a.m., then to the gym each day, enjoy coffee together at 10 a.m., lunch at a local café at 1 p.m., followed by a walk with the dog at 2 p.m., and Bill to the golf course at around 3 p.m. to get in nine holes. See, totally boring.

When Bill and Maru are not relaxing at home they have been on the road. The highlight was their two glorious weeks in Europe visiting Prague, Vienna, and Budapest. All three were great, but Budapest was special. They had heard that the thermal baths rejuvenate you and as they were retired, well semi-retired, well on sabbatical (hell, you get the picture) they felt some rejuvenation would be a good thing. They went to the Gellert Hotel, which was the inspiration of the movie,

Another Interesting Year

The Grand Budapest Hotel. It was so relaxing, and they never felt so young...never mind that they were the only guests in the pools that did not require a walker or wheelchair. In retrospect, this place was clearly also the basis for the movie, *Cocoon* as well.

Over the years, certain events have led Bill and Maru to question their parenting skills such as the time they accidently packed Billy to school with a can of beer when he was in kindergarten (honest mistake), but now there is additional and irrefutable proof. They managed to lose Tobi in a New York City hotel and did not even notice.

When they checked out and Tobi was with them, the front manager said, "Oh you're the owners of the white dog that people were calling me about!" He noted that guests saw him wondering the halls and someone even rode the elevator with him. He was also spotted in the breakfast area which explains the egg sandwich he had in his mouth when they saw him coming down the hall as they were leaving the room to check out. In all candor, they forgot he was with them. They assume he followed Bill out when he went for a morning run three hours earlier. Maru admits to hearing some noises in the hallway at one point, but thought it was the maid. Bill returned with muffins and coffee and they watched the Sunday morning news programs oblivious that he was gone.

In their defense, they don't normally travel with Tobi so it is understandable that they forgot about him; and besides, they always claimed to raise independent children who can survive on their own, so actually, another job well done! And while we are on the topic of his dramas, he once again wound up in Tufts Veterinary Hospital.

During the summer, he was rushed to the hospital because he was violently shaking non-stop. A thousand heart tests and two days of hospital care later they diagnosed him as "nervous." It seems that Ali's new six-pound emotional support dog, Alfie, who was staying with us for a week, gave our Tobi a nervous breakdown. Bill had his own mini breakdown too when they handed him the hospital bill. Both were prescribed Valium.

Onto the kids. They are doing well. Ali is back in acting school and on the honor role, getting roles in independent films, and plans to move to LA in June. As mentioned, she got a wonderful little dog, Alfie, who is a great addition to the family even if he terrorizes Tobi. Billy graduates high school this January and plans to live and work in New York City, then to college or more work; still to be decided, but he is happy and excited.

Now things are really pretty darn good. Odds are this year is an anomaly, but hell, even we think we are entitled to a year free of drama now and then. Again, sorry for those of you who anticipated something meatier. This concludes our letter.

To all our dear friends we wish you God's blessings for a happy holiday season and a peaceful and prosperous 2018!

Bill, Maru, Ali, and Billy

Another Interesting Year

CHRISTMAS 2018

To All Our Friends,
Greetings from Colorado! Yes, this is late, sorry. It has been an interesting year. The only thing that did not happen in 2018 was a hospital visit (Yay!) and given all the change we have all gone through that would have put us over the edge. Bill got a new job resulting in a move to the Denver area. Ali switched schools and moved to Hollywood to continue working on her career. Billy graduated high school and is starting college in Santa Barbara in a few weeks and Maru got a new set of teeth. It was a year of transitions for all.

Bill is now working for a company in Denver. That meant a move, but it was a great opportunity and with the kids kind of out of the house (but still on the dole unfortunately) we decided "what the hell" and we went for it. We gave up blizzards for hailstorms, and squirrels for rattle snakes, bears and bobcats all of which roam freely in our backyard along with herds of deer.

On the very positive side, the deer are Lyme free and there are no mosquitos! We miss our New England friends, but the people here are indeed warm and hospitable, there are three hundred days of sunshine annually, golf eleven months of the year, great skiing two hours away and we love the new house. Overall, it is pretty darn good.

The move has clearly shown us examples of what is wrong with our economic system. We are good with money. We have no debt, no mortgage left on the house in Medfield, no car payments, and a good income—so of course we had trouble getting a mortgage for the new house. Apparently since Bill was the co-signer of Ali's lease it made us a bad risk.

Ali, upon hearing that providing her with a place to live was preventing the rest of us from getting one, decided to go to her landlord to see if she could take Bill off of her lease. The landlord called Bill and said, "If we take you off and run a credit report on Ali and it is bad, it makes her credit rating even worse." Bill hears Ali in the background saying, "I don't even know what that means so go ahead."

Due to Ali, who didn't even have enough money on her debit card to buy a Halloween costume the week before, we got our mortgage. Somehow between her summer waitressing job and the meager royalties from her almost hit record she has an excellent credit rating. Hence, in today's America you need to be broke to be in good financial standing. No wonder the market is going to hell.

In other news, Maru's career is taking off too. She was asked to be a pornography photographer. We were at a hotel bar getting dinner and a drink while at a wedding in Florida and Maru, being Maru, started to chat up the bartender and she happened to mention that she was into photography. The bartender proceeded to tell Maru that she had an idea for a nature calendar and wanted to know if Maru might be interested in helping her pull it together. Maru, extremely excited about the potential of her first paying photography gig, said she would love to be involved.

Then Tammy, the bartender, told Maru she envisioned a nature scene where a young, bald weightlifter rips her shirt off against a tree (that was for the month of April) under the theme "Spring has sprung" and then May had her straddling a guy on a Harley, "Riding High." Tammy clearly had done her pre-work. Bill jumped in and said he always handles the wardrobe for Maru's shoots! Maru grabbed the bill with one hand and Bill by the earlobe with the other, and with that her pornography career and Bill's opportunity to attend a porn shoot ended abruptly, damn!!

Maru also got a new set of choppers after years of dental issues which started from birth, literally. She was born with teeth and they have been an issue ever since. She got her mother's small mouth and her dad's large teeth. Years of braces resulted in a very nice smile and then came Murphy the dog.

Shortly after they were engaged, Maru was meeting Bill's best friends for the first time and they had this ridiculous dog that jumped like a reindeer. He leaped and bumped Maru so hard that he busted her jaw. Maru didn't say anything when it happened because she was trying to make a good impression, but mostly because she couldn't talk. Years of dental work did nothing and Maru finally bit the bullet (every pun intended) and had a whole new set of teeth put in.

During Bill's sabbatical, Maru convinced him that they should take ballroom dancing classes. Bill finally gave in and he is so glad he did. Maru with her Latin blood was convinced she was going to be awesome. She sucked. She couldn't help herself, but everything she danced came out looking like a Salsa; she just couldn't stop her hips from swinging and swaying.

Bill on the other hand was a model student. Seems knowing nothing is good. He just listened to the coach, three steps this way, pivot, two steps to the side, pivot back—easy peasy— you have a Rumba! Maru would take off in some other direction after three steps this way. And dudes reading this, THE GUY GETS TO LEAD!! It is awesome. And if the gal tries to lead, the instructor yells at her. And since the whole thing is her idea there is nothing she can do. What a blissful hour a week.

We hope you are all well and that you have a happy and healthy 2019.

Merry Christmas!

Bill, Maru, Ali, and Billy

2018

Another Interesting Year

CHRISTMAS 2019

To All Our Friends,

Greetings from Colorado! It has been another interesting year of settling in, travel and typical Fox family adventures. The medical patient award once again goes to Bill this year. He made an agreement with Maru when they moved to Denver that he would continue to have his check-ups in Boston (frankly, way too many medical records to move). Anyway, he had to see his neurosurgeon for an annual check-up and managed to get diagnosed with an abdominal hernia. New city, same old Bill.

The kids are doing well and growing into responsible young adults (as of this writing). Billy is in college in Santa Barbara. He has been working hard at it and enjoys the school and the friends he has made but is still not sure if college is for him, so he is teetering on returning or looking for work. In any event, he is doing well. Ali is still in Hollywood, trying to make it as an actress, but her side job as a waitress in the meantime is going great and she was promoted to "technical trainer" which both thrilled and shocked us (and Ali) and we are proud that her efforts are being rewarded with some base line managerial responsibilities. She is also studying film editing as a plan B. Yay!

On the settling into the Denver area part, we have to say we love Coloradans. Wonderful, friendly, salt of the earth people. But they are all liars. The three hundred plus days of sunshine that they boast about is a total lie and they are all in on it. It was one of the attractions they lured us in with when Bill was being recruited last year. Utter nonsense. It starts snowing in October (four significant storms thus far and it isn't officially winter yet). We were told last year, "It's just a fluke," but here we are again. It's no damn fluke.

We suspect they had three hundred days of sunshine once, more than a decade ago, and then they immediately started a PR campaign, printed bumper stickers and changed all the brochures in their travel offices and on their campus recruiting materials. Subsequently, businesses started flocking here which meant more tourists and housing starts; house values started to climb and so there was no turning back; kind of a weather Ponzi scheme and we are in on it now (our housing value depends on it).

So, when people ask, "When is a good time to visit?" we drank the Kool-Aid and gleefully say, "Virtually any time. The weather is perfect year-round!" But for the people we really like, we say, "May or September," the rest is just a crapshoot.

One very plus side of living in the Denver area is the proximity to some incredible natural wonders. We have enjoyed easy, incredibly scenic car trips to Mount Rushmore, the Colorado Sand Dunes, The Grand Tetons, and Yellowstone Park. Yellowstone was incredible and we decided to get back to nature, so we camped there. We spent four days sleeping in a tent and we found it surprisingly nice. Okay, most of you know we are not really the camping type, so relax, we haven't totally gone crazy with the western move. Our style of camping is actually staying in a hotel room which happens to be under a tent complete with king sized bed, a wood burning stove and a minibar with cocktails. We are now camping converts.

One of the goals in the park is to sight the four big animal attractions, bison, elk, wolves, and bears. Bison are initially amazing, but then you quickly find that they are as plentiful as pigeons in New York City and by day two they are nothing but an annoyance that blocks traffic. The big attraction which every visitor from around the globe is on the hunt for (figuratively) is the black bear. We quickly got bear fever, especially Maru.

Every time Maru sensed a bear in the area, Bill would practically have to careen off the road while Maru got out her camera and shot thousands of phots with the hopes that one of them captured a bear in the distance. Then it happened— a true bear sighting. Tears of joy ran down her face; a bucket list item crossed off, tee shirts stating, "We Sighted a Bear" bought; we went home to Denver fulfilled.

Two days later what's in our backyard, but a damn bear, lapping up water from our fountain. One thousand miles of driving, car alignment ruined on unpaved back roads, and we could have had a better bear experience while having a gin and tonic in our backyard.

Another new experience for Bill and Maru was living through an avalanche, well actually two. We rented a place in the "high country" for a week where we could ski, snowshoe and dog sled (yes, we are embracing it all). On our third night,

Another Interesting Year

and without checking the weather forecast, we went for a wonderful dinner at the top of Vail and on what should have been a twenty minute drive back to the condo, an avalanche drove through the highway in front of us, followed quickly by a second one that came in behind us.

It took two hours for emergency crews to finally get close enough to let us know that they were aware that we were stuck and doing their best to get us free. At six hours trapped, we both later admitted that our exhausted minds were each wondering who was going to eat the other first. Finally, salvation came after seven hours.

Three days later, on our way home, we were blocked in by yet another avalanche, but being experienced mountaineers at this point, the four hours was barely daunting. We also were smart enough to load the car with water and granola bars just in case.

On a sad note, we lost Bill's mom earlier this year. Her health was failing and the ravages of that dreaded disease, Alzheimer's was starting to set in, so in many ways it was a blessing as she left with her dignity in place. For that we are very grateful.

We hope you are all well and we send you blessings for a happy and healthy 2020!

Merry Christmas!

Bill, Maru, Ali, and Billy

Another Interesting Year

CHRISTMAS 2020

To All Our Friends,

It has been another interesting year for the Fox family full of travel, intrigue, new jobs for the kids and a Covid-19 diagnosis for Bill (come on, you knew that was going to happen). The year started off great. Bill had a business trip to India in February and taking advantage of the fact that he would be there a week, he arranged to spend another week there where Maru joined him for a tour of many of the historic sights. Most of the time was spent in Delhi and they took in all the major attractions, but the Taj Mahal was as special as it was expected to be. Just magnificent. Maru kept reminding Bill that he built this in tribute to his wife. Bill reminded Maru that he promised her he would build a mosque in her honor on her death bed as she gave birth to his nineteenth child. We only have two, so our house is proportional. On our way back, it was clear the world was entering a crisis. We could sense it traveling, the Coronavirus was starting to take hold and even some Chinese tourists wore masks. This was the end of February and the beginning of the end of life as we knew it.

Crisis hit Bill in March. It started with a visit to see Oprah. Bill very considerately bought Maru two tickets to see Oprah on her Denver stop of her national tour as her Christmas present, thinking she would want to take a friend. Instead, she insisted on taking Bill. She promised there would be thousands of guys there with their wives. There were fifteen. We know this because Oprah got on stage and asked that a spotlight shine on the fifteen brave men in the audience of fifteen thousand. Bill and his testicles shrunk to the floor immediately. The women seated around us started to chant, "He's over here! We have one," and the spotlight found him as did the jumbotron. It was unquestionably the most embarrassing moment of his life, and he has had his share of embarrassing moments.

The following week Bill went to Vail skiing, took on moguls and double black diamond trails in an attempt to regain his masculinity, but he came down with Covid instead. Diagnosed on March 17th, a relatively early case and fortunately only one night at the hospital. And while it was a miserable three weeks, he has made a full recovery. But this is Bill and he got reinfected in November, of course.

We came to a monumental conclusion. Some people are beach oriented, others lake and mountains. We are sewer people. We love our home, but it is the first time we have lived in a house with a septic tank. So far it has backed up twice, and before you all go there, we are not that full of crap. The septic technicians claim that we are just unlucky (understatement). We had also heard that grass grows greener over the septic tank. Not in our case. In fact, we cannot grow grass there or anywhere else. We spent a fortune on hydroseeding, and Maru was outside four times a day watering and all we got was a patch of grass you could cover with a placemat. This went on for six weeks and then we gave up, and now we have a lot of growth which the locals call "native grass" which is

Coloradan for weeds. We are locals now.

The kids are doing well. Billy is a full-fledged productive member of society. He is working full time at a nice country club and loves it. He has made some great friends and is finally considering Colorado home. Ali was a struggling actress (a.k.a. full-time waitress) before Covid. She has shifted gears and has formed a small film production house and is actually making money at it. We would like to let you all know that your tax dollars that went into the CARES Act relief program that provided the extra $600 a week to Ali, went to buying all her production equipment and she thanks you and we do too.

It has been a crazy year and we cannot wait for it to be over. We are sure you all agree. We will hang in there and hope you all do too. Thanks for sharing in yet another year of our life and we look forward to sharing with you the next twenty. To all our dear friends, we wish you God's blessings for a wonderful and prosperous 2021!

Bill, Maru, Ali, and Billy

Another Interesting Year

ACKNOWLEDGMENTS

Special thanks to Joanne Davis for encouraging us to make this book happen, Cheryl Benton for making it happen, Miriam Otalvo and Mary Andrews Brown for helping us find the elusive letter, and Kevin Guill for helping to market the book.

ABOUT THE FOXES

Bill and Maru Fox currently live in the Denver metropolitan area. Bill is a marketing executive and Maru is a biochemical engineer and CEO of the family. They have raised two children, Ali and Billy, and two dogs, Tobi and Alfie to adulthood. They love to travel and have been to over fifty countries. Bill has run a couple of marathons and plays golf (poorly). Maru loves Zumba, water aerobics, and photography. They have logged in enough hours in emergency rooms to qualify for gold upgrade status. They are well known for their holiday parties, Christmas letters, Maru's guacamole and her corn casserole, and Bill's Kahlua cake.

www.ingramcontent.com/pod-product-compliance
Lightning Source LLC
Chambersburg PA
CBHW071003080526
44587CB00015B/2326